T0063665

SPACEBUSTERS RACE TO THE MOON

FIRST EDITION
Project Editor Penny Smith; **Designer** Andrew Burgess; **Series Editor** Deborah Lock;
Managing Art Editor Martin Wilson; **US Editor** Regina Kahney; **Production Editor** Sarah Isle;
Picture Researcher Jo Carlill; **Illustrator** Peter Dennis; **Jacket Designer** Natalie Godwin;
Reading Consultant Linda Gambrell, PhD

THIS EDITION
Editorial Management by Oriel Square
Produced for DK by WonderLab Group LLC
Jennifer Emmett, Erica Green, Kate Hale, *Founders*

Editors Grace Hill Smith, Libby Romero, Michaela Weglinski;
Photography Editors Kelley Miller, Annette Kiesow, Nicole DiMella; **Managing Editor** Rachel Houghton;
Designers Project Design Company; **Researcher** Michelle Harris; **Copy Editor** Lori Merritt;
Indexer Connie Binder; **Proofreader** Larry Shea; **Reading Specialist** Dr. Jennifer Albro;
Curriculum Specialist Elaine Larson

Published in the United States by DK Publishing
1745 Broadway, 20th Floor, New York, NY 10019

23 24 25 26 27 10 9 8 7 6 5 4 3 2 1
001–333463–Apr/2023

Published in Great Britain by Dorling Kindersley Limited

A catalog record for this book
is available from the Library of Congress.
HC ISBN: 978-0-7440-6824-5
PB ISBN: 978-0-7440-6825-2

Printed and bound in China

The publisher would like to thank the following for their kind permission to reproduce their images:
a=above; c=center; b=below; l=left; r=right; t=top; b/g=background

Alamy Stock Photo: The Picture Art Collection 11br; **NASA:** 9t, 30crb, 32t, JSC 24crb;
Shutterstock.com: Eric Broder Van Dyke 40crb, Polina Valentina 18-19b

Cover images: *Front:* **Dreamstime.com:** Peter Jurik / Pitris (BG)

For the curious
www.dk.com

Level 3

SPACEBUSTERS

RACE TO THE MOON

Philip Wilkinson

DK

Contents

Journey to the Moon

Three, two, one—blastoff! With a great roar, the Apollo 11 rocket lifted off the ground. Flames and smoke poured from its base as it started its dangerous journey to the Moon.

President John F. Kennedy had promised an American would reach the Moon before the end of the 1960s. It was already the summer of 1969. The astronauts could make history!

But Commander Neil Armstrong's heart pounded. He and his crew had only a 50-50 chance of actually landing on the moon during this first attempt.

Takeoff, July 16, 1969
The three astronauts were, from left to right, Neil Armstrong, Michael Collins, and Edwin (Buzz) Aldrin.

Armstrong kept an eye on the instrument panel. He watched the lights and dials change as the rocket quickly picked up speed.

Soon, they were traveling 25,000 miles per hour (40,200 kph)—thirty times faster than a jet plane. The force pushed the astronauts back into their seats and made it hard to move.

The entire spacecraft was as tall as a skyscraper. Most of this was a rocket that held fuel. When the fuel was used up, the astronauts released the rocket and continued their journey in a capsule called the Command Module.

Releasing the Rocket

After nearly 12 minutes, the rocket, now empty of fuel, broke away and fell to the ground.

Commander Neil Armstrong

Armstrong turned to talk to Aldrin. It would take three days to reach the Moon, and Armstrong wanted to go over their planned landing.

Aldrin had spent years studying space. He looked forward to walking on the Moon and doing experiments there.

While Armstrong and Aldrin worked, the third astronaut, Michael Collins, got himself something to eat. Since everything in the spacecraft was weightless, ordinary food would float off a plate. Collins had to eat what looked like baby food from a plastic bag.

All the food had been dried to store it for the journey, so it had to be mixed with water. But there was plenty of choice, including beef and chicken.

Human Computers

Before computers were invented, people did calculations themselves. Dorothy Johnson Vaughan led a crew of female African American mathematicians, known as human computers. They did all of the calculations that helped the astronauts get to the moon.

Dorothy Johnson Vaughan

As the spacecraft sped toward the Moon, the three astronauts rested. They needed to save their energy so they would be wide awake for the dangers of the Moon landing ahead.

Out in space, the Sun's heat is fierce. The capsule turned around and around. This stopped it from getting too hot on one side and burning up.

Sometimes, when the astronauts looked out the windows, they could see Earth. It was shining brightly and looked like a beautiful, giant disk in the sky.

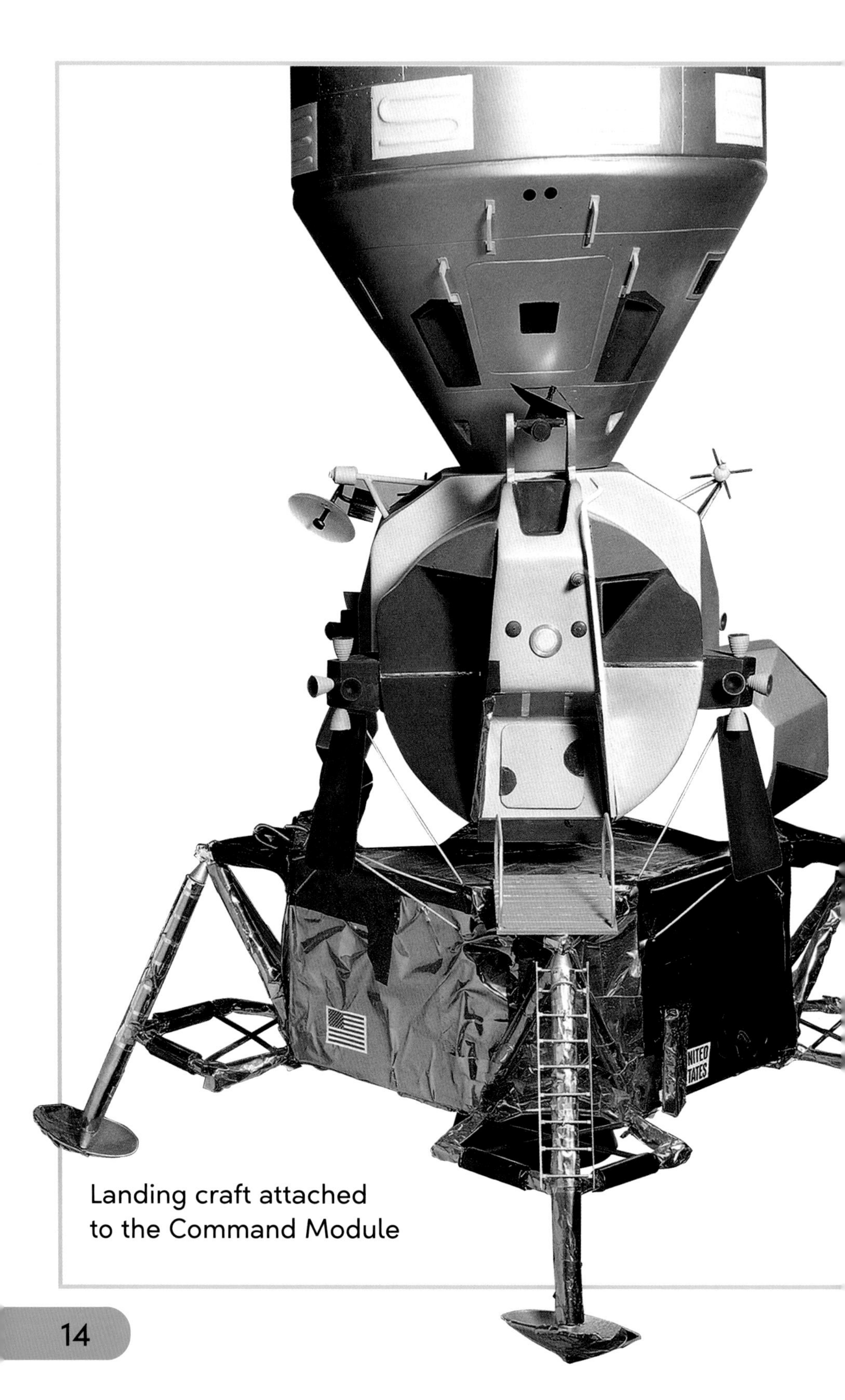

Landing craft attached to the Command Module

The astronauts planned to set down on an area of the Moon called the Sea of Tranquility (tran-KWILL-it-ee). It was not a real sea because there is no water on the Moon.

From Earth, the Sea of Tranquility looked like a flat plain—a good surface to land on.

The spacecraft circled the Moon once, sending pictures back to Earth. Then, the big moment arrived. It was time for two of the astronauts to try to land.

Armstrong and Aldrin prepared to leave the Command Module and enter the small landing craft that would take them to the Moon. They climbed through the craft's narrow hatch. The craft was nicknamed the *Eagle*, but it looked more like a giant metal spider.

Collins stayed in the Command Module and pressed a button. Slowly, the two crafts separated. Then, the *Eagle* headed for the Moon's surface with its passengers on board.

As Armstrong and Aldrin drew close, they could see the surface more clearly.

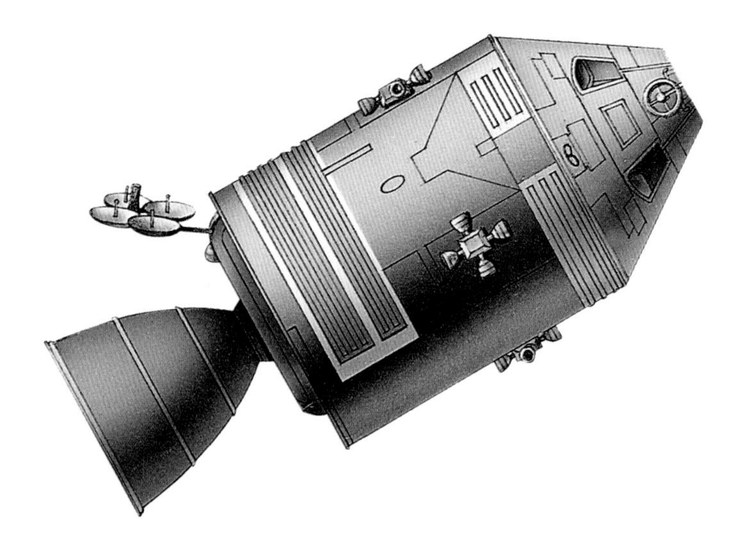

The Moon did not look flat enough to land on. It was peppered with craters and covered in boulders the size of small cars. They could not see a smooth place to set down!

The *Eagle* came closer and closer to the Moon. It was steered by a computer. But this computer could not see the dangerous surface ahead. It kept them straight on course. They were going to crash-land in a huge crater!

Armstrong grabbed the controls and began to fly the landing craft manually.

Steering the Landing Craft
Sixteen small rockets spaced around the landing craft were used to make the craft move right or left, up or down.

"How's the fuel?" he asked Aldrin.

"Eight percent," Aldrin replied. This meant there was very little fuel left. They had only seconds to land!

Mission Control
Scientists directed the flight from Mission Control in Texas, USA. The person who spoke to the astronauts was called the CapCom.

Armstrong spotted a smooth place to land. Quickly, he began to bring the craft straight down. Moon dust flew everywhere, and Armstrong could not see where they were going.

Then, he heard Aldrin say, “Contact light.” They were down! Armstrong hit the button marked “Engine Stop.” Then, he radioed Mission Control on Earth. “The *Eagle* has landed,” he announced.

One Giant Leap

Armstrong wanted to get out and explore the Moon right away. But he knew it was important to check the spacecraft first. He and Aldrin needed to make it ready for takeoff. If they met some unknown danger, they might have to leave the Moon in a hurry.

When the craft was ready, they helped each other put on their outside clothing. They pulled on overshoes. Then, they put on helmets with visors to deflect the Sun's blinding light.

Spacesuit

A spacesuit is like a miniature spacecraft. It has everything the astronaut needs to survive outside the craft, such as a radio, oxygen, and watertight pouches to store urine. The astronauts can even sip drinks inside their suits.

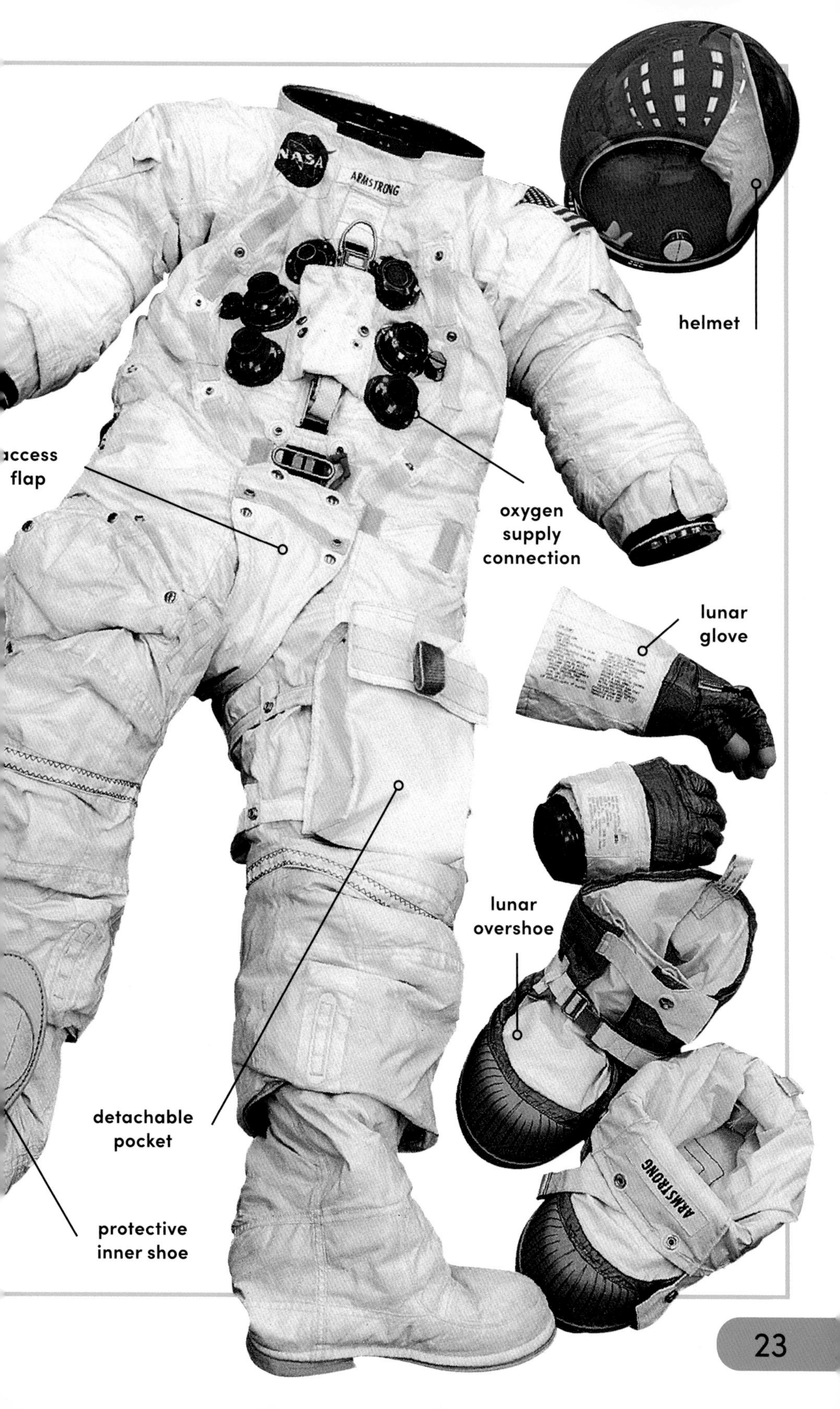
NASA
ARMSTRONG
helmet
access flap
oxygen supply connection
lunar glove
lunar overshoe
detachable pocket
protective inner shoe
ARMSTRONG

Each astronaut also wore a huge backpack. It contained an oxygen supply so he could breathe. The packs were heavy, but everything is lighter on the Moon because there is less gravity, so they could carry them with ease.

"All set for gloves?" Aldrin asked. Once these were on, the spacesuits were complete.

Then, each astronaut flicked a switch. Motors in the backpacks began to hum. Aldrin felt a whoosh on his face as oxygen filled his helmet. They were ready to go outside.

The Force of Gravity

This force holds people on the ground. When people experience the extremely low gravity of being in orbit, they feel lighter and can float.

Cameras in the landing craft sent pictures back to Mission Control on Earth. As the scientists watched, Armstrong pushed the hatch open and stepped through the gap.

Armstrong climbed carefully down the nine rungs toward the Moon's surface. He could see that the Moon was covered in a light dust. "It's almost like powder," he said into his radio to Mission Control. He hoped his feet would find firm ground.

Then, he stepped off the last rung. Under the dust, the ground was hard. Armstrong was very happy. He was the first human being ever to stand on the Moon. His next words were heard all over the world. "That's one small step for man, one giant leap for mankind."

The World Watches
An estimated 650 million people around the world watched on television as Armstrong took his "one small step" onto the moon.

Armstrong looked over the bleak and barren landscape. Then, he raised his camera and took some photographs.

A scoop was used to collect rocks.

Next, he bent over to collect samples for scientists on Earth. He filled a bag with dust, adding some rocks for good measure.

Armstrong was overjoyed. He had collected one bag of Moon samples. Now it was time for some fun. He threw away the handle of the collecting bag. Even with a gentle underarm throw, the handle traveled a long way. The Moon's gravity was too weak to pull it down.

Aldrin stayed in the landing craft. He watched his friend playing on the Moon's surface. "I didn't know you could throw so far," he joked.

Landing Craft Feet
The landing craft had wide feet to stop it from sinking into the Moon. Gold foil helped protect the feet from the cold.

Aldrin was itching to join Armstrong. At last it was his turn. Aldrin climbed slowly down the landing craft ladder and stepped onto the Moon. He looked down. Wherever he put his boots, he left clear, sharp footprints.

Together, Aldrin and Armstrong planted the American flag. It was hard to push the flag into the Moon's rough surface. But once it was up, the astronauts stood next to it and felt proud.

Footprints
There is no wind or rain on the Moon, so the astronauts' footprints will remain there forever.

Aldrin decided to try running. He made huge strides and bounded like a kangaroo. But he felt as though he was running in slow motion.

Aldrin stands next to the American flag, which was stiffened with wire because there is no wind on the Moon.

The astronauts got busy—there was work to be done! First, they set up a machine that was able to detect any movements on the Moon's surface.

Measuring Instrument
This showed that it's 240,000 miles (390,000 km) from the Earth to the Moon. That's more than nine times around the world.

The machine would send this information back to Earth. They also set up an instrument to help scientists measure the distance from Earth to the Moon.

The astronauts worked for two and a half hours, then returned to the *Eagle* to rest. They had to be alert to take off and dock with the Command Module, which was orbiting the Moon. One mistake and they could drift off into space and be lost forever.

Armstrong and Aldrin climbed into the landing craft and closed the hatch. They were covered in Moon dust. Some scientists had said the dust would catch fire in oxygen. But the astronauts needed oxygen to breathe. They turned on the air supply and waited. The cabin filled with air. But the dust was safe. It did not ignite.

The astronauts tried to rest, but they were too keyed up about liftoff. Collins was circling around the Moon. Would they ever see him again?

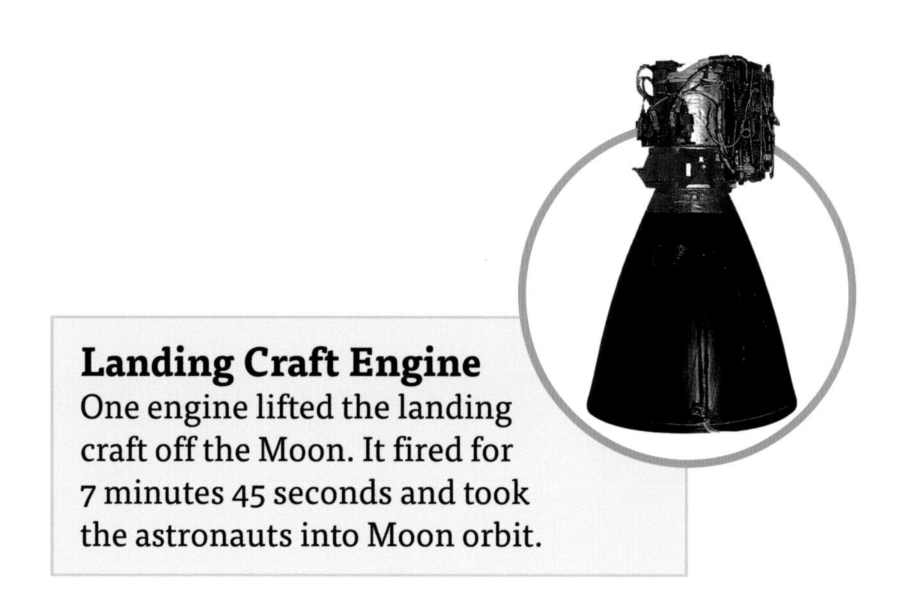

Landing Craft Engine
One engine lifted the landing craft off the Moon. It fired for 7 minutes 45 seconds and took the astronauts into Moon orbit.

When it was finally time to leave the Moon, Aldrin hit the button marked "proceed." The engine fired up. Moon dust and debris sprayed all around them. They were off!

The landing craft left its legs behind at takeoff.

Homeward Bound

While Armstrong and Aldrin were exploring, Collins circled the Moon in the Command Module. For half of each orbit, he was on the far side of the Moon—the side always turned away from Earth. Everything was silent. No radio signals could reach him. Collins was completely out of contact with the rest of the human race. No one had ever been more alone.

Collins was worried that Armstrong and Aldrin would get stuck on the Moon, or that they wouldn't be able to dock with the Command Module. If either happened, he would have to leave his two friends in space.

The Command Module orbiting the Moon

At last, through his window, Collins spotted the landing craft coming toward him. He steered the Command Module carefully so that the two crafts lined up ready for docking.

The spacecrafts were almost touching. One false move and they could miss each other completely.

Seconds seemed like hours. Then, a buzzer sounded, and a set of latches closed with a clunk. The landing craft had attached to the Command Module.

Armstrong and Aldrin clambered back into the module. At last, Collins could relax. They could all return to Earth together.

It would take three days for the astronauts to reach Earth. They caught up on their sleep on the long journey home.

At last, they entered Earth's atmosphere—the layer of air around the planet. Then, the outside of the spacecraft began to heat up. It became 25 times hotter than a kitchen oven.

The spacecraft was protected by a heat shield. Through the window, the astronauts could see bits of the shield come off and fly past them. They prayed that the shield would hold out.

Heat Shield
Metals light enough for a spacecraft could not resist great heat. So, the craft was coated with resin that would burn away and keep it cool.

Crack! The astronauts heard the noise of the first small parachutes, called the drogues, opening above them. The drogues set the craft on an even keel, so that it would fall steadily down to Earth.

Whoosh! A small vent opened, bringing air into the cabin. This made the air inside the craft the same as it was on the outside.

Then, there was another cracking sound. The main parachutes opened. Now they were floating slowly down. Finally, with a loud splash, they landed in the Pacific Ocean.

The pickup crew found them floating in the water several minutes later.

Back on land, the astronauts had to be kept apart from other people. They stayed in a special laboratory to make sure they hadn't brought back any germs from the Moon.

After about two weeks, the doctors said the astronauts were all in good health. They were let out of their small room, and returned home to their families.
Mission accomplished!

The Later Years

After Apollo 11, there were six more Apollo missions to the Moon. Some of the astronauts on these missions explored the Moon using a small, battery-powered car called a Lunar Rover.

In 1981, a new spacecraft blasted off—the Space Shuttle. Unlike the Apollo rockets, the Shuttle was reusable. Its huge cargo hold carried scientific equipment into space to do work that would be impossible to do on Earth.

The Hubble Space Telescope has been repaired in space by Shuttle astronauts. It provides fascinating images of space.

Neil Armstrong taught aerospace engineering at the University of Cincinnati, Ohio, USA. He then moved to a farm in his native Ohio. He died on August 25, 2012.

Lunar Rover

Astronauts have now lived in orbiting space stations for months at a time. Spacecraft from Earth have reached the outer limits of our solar system.

The next step? The possibilities are endless—perhaps astronauts on Mars!

Edwin (Buzz) Aldrin became a space engineer, designing spacecraft and planning future missions.

Michael Collins became a director of the National Air and Space Museum in Washington, DC, USA. He died on April 28, 2021.

Glossary

Apollo 11
The spacecraft used to land a human on the Moon for the first time

Astronauts
Men and women who have been trained to travel in space

Atmosphere
The layer of air or other gases that surrounds Earth and other planets

CapCom
The person at Mission Control who talks directly to the astronauts. CapCom is short for Capsule Communicator.

Command Module
The part of the spacecraft where the astronauts lived and worked during their journey from Earth to the Moon

Docking
The joining together of two spacecrafts in space

Drogues
Three small parachutes that steadied the spacecraft as it fell to Earth

Gravity
The force that pulls things toward the ground and holds them there

Heat shield
A protective covering on the outside of the Command Module. The shield kept the craft cool as it neared Earth.

Laboratory
A room or building where scientific experiments are performed

Landing craft
The spacecraft that the astronauts used to land on the Moon's surface

Mission Control
A place in Houston, Texas, USA, from which scientists direct space flights and advise astronauts

Orbit
The path taken when one body circles around another body, such as when Earth goes around the Sun

Space
The vast area around and beyond Earth that contains the planets and stars

Spacecraft
Any vehicle that is designed for travel in space

Weightless
The lack of gravitational pull in space that allows objects to float

Index

Quiz

Answer the questions to see what you have learned. Check your answers in the key below.

1. In what year did Apollo 11 blast off?
2. How long did it take to reach the Moon?
3. What was the nickname of the landing craft?
4. What did Armstrong say the Moon was covered in?
5. What did Armstrong say when he stepped on the Moon?
6. What was Collins doing while Aldrin and Armstrong were on the Moon?
7. What protected the spacecraft as it entered Earth's atmosphere?
8. Where did the astronauts land on Earth?

1. 1969 2. Three days 3. The *Eagle* 4. A light dust
5. "That's one small step for man, and one giant leap for mankind"
6. Circling the Moon in the Command Module 7. A heat shield
8. The Pacific Ocean